Sister Code

This book is a work of non-fiction. Names, characters, places, and incidents are the product of the author's life stories.

Sister Code the book © 2018 The Valley Girls Productions and all character names and their distinctive likenesses © 2018
All Rights Reserved

In accordance with the U.S. Copyright Act of 1976 the scanning, uploading, and electronic sharing of any part of this book without permission of the publisher is unlawful piracy and theft of the author's intellectual property. If you would like to use material from the book (other than for review purposes), prior written permission must be obtained by contacting the publisher at rodprattpresents@gmail.com
Thank you for your support of the author's rights.

Roderick Pratt

The publisher is not responsible for websites (or their content) that are not owned by the publisher.

First Edition: April 2018

ISBN 8339627
Printed In The United States of America

SISTER CODE

Written by
Dakai, Diya & Dumia Valley

Illustration by Ada Ezenwa-Autrey
Artwork by Triggy Herrington
Edited by Amber Farrar
Originally published by Roderick Pratt

Chapter 1: Sisterhood Diya

Chapter 2: Listen, Learn, Love Dakai

Chapter 3: Make New Friends But Keep The Old Dumia

Chapter 4: Love Yourself Girl Or Nobody Will Dumia

Chapter 5: Black Girl Magic Dakai

Chapter 6: A Valuable Lesson Diya

Chapter 7: Want To Win Dumia

Chapter 8: Count Your Blessings Dakai

Chapter 9: Love The Skin You're In Diya

Chapter 10: Honor The Code Dumia

Foreword

This is Haley from Page Parkes. I believe in these girls. They are all stars - I believe it wholeheartedly. I don't usually feel *this* strongly about everyone I encounter. Diya has sass and charisma for days. She's charming on and off camera - she's so kind, includes the class and includes her sisters, everyday and is beautiful to watch on-camera. She is a commercial talent through and through. Dumia is quirky, spunky, and smart. She's hilarious and honest and isn't afraid to be herself. It's so refreshing to see that in someone so young - she has a strength that is so rare (being yourself is hard!)! I could see her rocking a sitcom or comedy show. Improv is a friend to her! Dakai is poised, loving, mature, and yet silly. She is a team player, and she's non-judgmental. She's wise beyond her years but is vulnerable enough to laugh at herself. She truly has a knack for being on film and would be beautiful in a drama. Each girl is unique, beautiful, and destined for incredible things. I believe in their personalities and their passionate hearts and they are stars in my eyes. No matter where they go in life, I am a forever fan.

Thank you for sharing them with us at Page Parkes.

Haley Hussey

Actress/Wardrobe Stylist

Acknowledgements

With every ounce of tough love, motivation, and encouragement instilled in us from our Mommy, Granny, Great Grandma Dorothy, Great-Great Grandma Margarette, Aunt Pookie, Great Aunt Bernice, Antwoinese, Re-Re, Missy, Sassy, Sani, Aubree, Tycen, Lyla, Dmijah, Lacee, Swayze, Coach Wanda, Ms. Lillian, Ms. Torrey, and so many other positive female influences we have gathered short stories, letters, and pages of notes as an outlet to help self-motivated girls just like us. This read is for to our little sisters who may need to know that us big sisters got your back. We are not perfect and face challenges every day-to-day, familiar to others. We hope this book serves a purpose to you.
With love,
The Valley Girls

Sister Code of Conduct: Help A Sister

H- Have

E- Empathy

L- Loyalty

P- Purpose

A- Ambition

S- Self Love

I- Identity

S- Smile

T- Trust

E- Encouragement

R- Respect

All these things are required to be the best you that you can be, so be them!

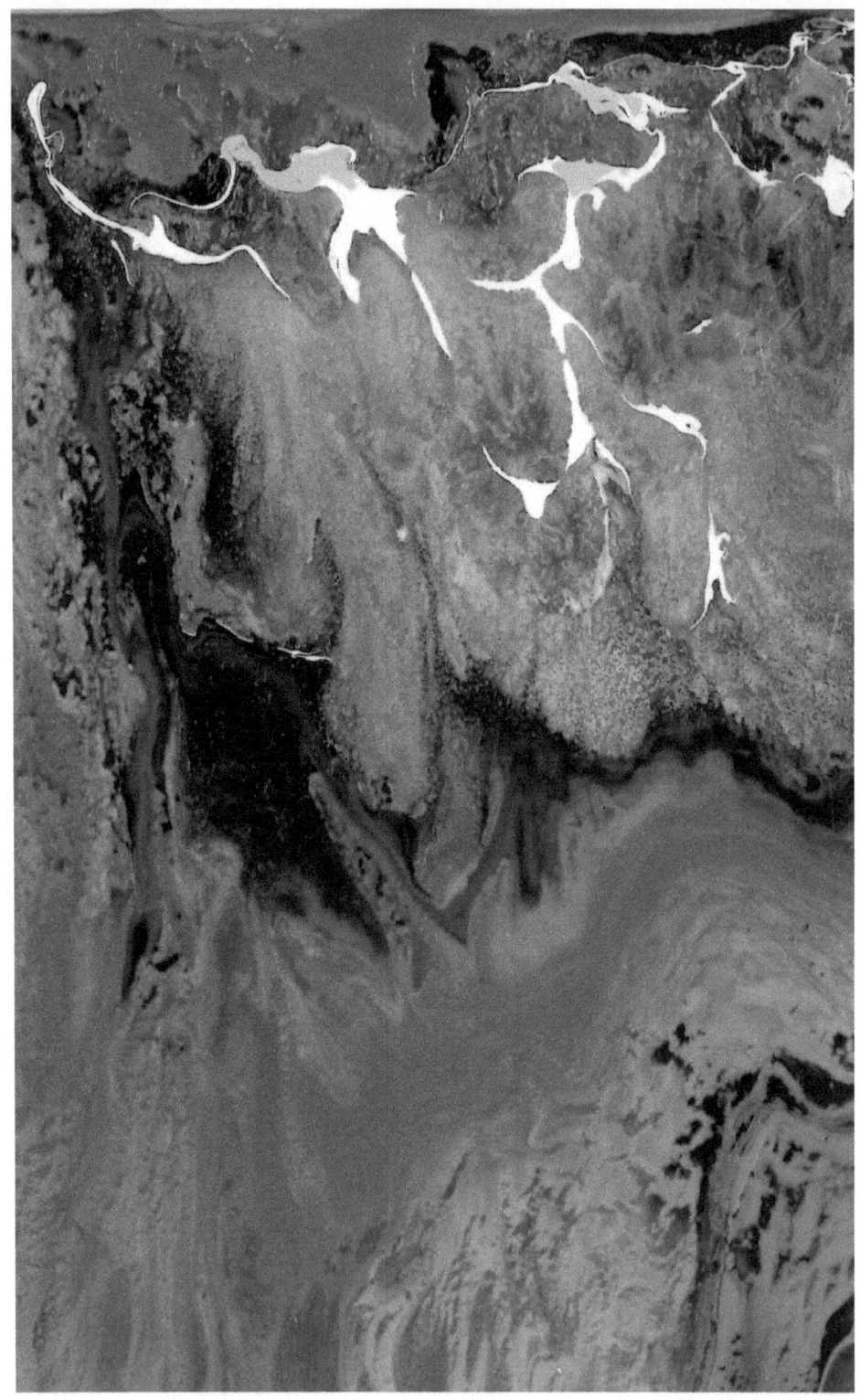

Chapter 1

Sisterhood

Sister | sis-ter |

A female regarded as a comrade.

My name is Diya, and I am 10 years old I have two sisters, Dakai who is 11 and Dumia who is 9 and I love and care about them very much. We're pretty much a package deal. We are so close that people think we are triplets sometimes. Dumia's the youngest, but she's much taller than I am so people mistake me as the youngest. Since we're together everywhere we go, people call us "The Valley Girls" instead of calling us out individually. At school over the loudspeaker we hear "Valley Girls for dismissal," at cheer practice when our friend's moms call us, they all say "The Valley Girls." We have very different personalities, and we don't always agree with everything, but at the end of the day, we're family. Surprisingly we argue and fuss about little things, but I think that's why we have a good bond. Our mom teaches us that it's ok to disagree. It's even ok to get upset because we're all human and we can't help how we feel sometimes. As long as whatever we do is with love the results of any situation will be ok. I love how funny my sisters are we joke about everything, even our arguments. We stick to the sister code by protecting each other, being trustworthy & understanding. I love them more than the sweetest candy on earth! That's love!

    Besides my three blood sisters, God blessed me with God sisters (McKiya and Mariya), my soul sister (Robyn), cousins that are like little sisters (Aubree & Tycen), also cheer friends, classmates from elementary, modeling and acting school that are my sisters for life! So just because your mom didn't birth girls, doesn't mean you can't create sister circles. Even if you don't have siblings at all this applies to you too. You can adopt a sister by becoming a part of a group or an organization that has an agenda as such. Sisters are very important. Girl groups are fun because females are full of creativity, spunk, and love! Everyone needs a sister no matter what gender or age you may be. Two minds are better than one, so having a friend that you don't mind listening to if you're right or wrong is the smart thing to do. My sisters motivate me, and we can relate to one another. We exchange good advice, and even if someone gives some not so useful information, we can learn from mistakes together. Achieving accomplishments together is a plus, because we have each other to celebrate with when we want!

My mom has five kids, my brother Amir is the oldest, and us girls recently became big sisters to a cute little fellow named Dalyn who helps us practice being impressive role models. I'm a little big sister literally. Being a good sister doesn't only apply to other sisters. Us girls have to stick together, but our brothers need us too. Brothers learn to love from sisters, and love is much needed. Being the middle sister is tough. I have to balance being the little sister that always listens, and being the big sister that leads by example. My life is complicated, but sure enough, I make the best of it. One thing for sure with all of our personalities in my house alone my people skills are entirely up to par.

Our mom makes us practice treating ourselves, and siblings with nothing but love no matter what. She also says that practice makes perfect so I think it's safe to say that I'm an excellent little big sister!

What are your goals as a sister?

_____

Name your blood sisters:

_____

Stepsisters:

_____

God sisters:

_____

Adopted sisters:

_____

Sister circles:

_____

How do you motivate your sisters?

_____

How do your sisters motivate you?

_____

Chapter 2

Listen, Learn, Love

Listen | lis•ten |

To hear something with thoughtful attention: give consideration.

Learn | lern |

To gain knowledge or understanding of or skill in by study, instruction, or experience.

Love | lev |

Unselfish loyal and benevolent

Listen

It is essential to listen to your big and little sisters because you can learn and accomplish so much more when you do so. Sisters are a good source for advice, compliments, and feedback. If you're a good listener, you will be able to dodge mistakes some of your sisters already made in their life, and if you do happen to make the same mistakes, you'll have your sister to help resolve them. Think about a time when you didn't listen, and you ended up regretting that.

Once, my little sister told me that when school was over, I needed to come straight home and not go to after school tutorials so that I could go to their school's First Family Dance. I was not paying attention to what they were saying, and I did not get to attend their school dance. That day I realized that I needed to focus and pay more attention to my little sisters so that I could have more fun and spend a bunch of time with them. My baby brother even went, and I missed pictures, pizza, and I heard there was a soul train line. My big brother Amir didn't listen either, so we lost that opportunity together. The reason I was most upset about missing the dance is that's what I love to do. Dancing is my life.

    I miss my dance instructor Redd at Coca in St Louis so much. Listening played a significant part in his class. I needed to listen to Redd, the beats of the songs, and my classmates to be able to connect in class and perform with advanced students. Everything we do will require listening.

Learn

When I was in St. Louis I was in a play called "Sweet Jenn." I was petrified until my drama teacher (Ms. Lakeitha) gave me so much advice and encouragement. I was so excited that out of anybody Ms. Lakeitha could have called to fill this role in a play that she wrote herself, she chose me. I listened very closely to her because she was obviously a professional, and I did amazing on my show. I even got paid a check for $100 for my roll performed at three local libraries and a community college. The goal I wanted to accomplish was to be confident like Ms. Lakeitha said, and I did it. Just by listening to everything she had coached me to do I was able to contribute to a successful show. I always accept advice or feedback from anyone to do better each time I perform.

My listening skill has contributed to my success in dance class, drama class, sewing class, modeling class, and school. Last year I met a terrific friend named Lyla Danh, who's become my big sister because she loves to help me with anything! Lyla and my 5th-grade teacher, Teeanna Kelly has helped me to stop second guessing myself and to believe in myself plus go outside the box. Ms. Kelly wrote me a note saying "Dakai! You are such a joy to have in class and you always work so hard! Ms. Kelly wants you to stop second-guessing yourself. You are brilliant, and I can tell that you put effort into studying. Always go with your first mind and don't doubt yourself! You will be able to get into any school that you wish to attend. Howard will be an amazing choice!" That note touched me, and from then on I have 100% faith in everything I do. I listened to these people that I named so I can learn and accomplish more.

It's going to be hard to learn anything from anybody if you always have your mouth open. A rule in our house is to listen and speak if necessary. Almost every time I was supposed to do something and didn't, wasn't because I didn't want to it was because I wasn't listening and I didn't know what was going on which always causes me to miss out because my mom never rewards you if you don't deserve it. I don't get mad, and I work on sharpening my skills.

Love

My Granny (Yolanda Campbell) talks on the phone with us almost every day and gives us more than advice to listen and learn from; she shares much love. She sets rules too. My Granny dislikes for us to call her Granny "Yolanda," but when I was little, she made us learn how to spell her name. My Granny is so funny that way, but only love could have you concerned with someone knowing how to spell something you don't want them to say. I make sure I take notes and learn from everything she says and teaches me because I know that it's all love. My Granny knows my sisters, and I love her so much! We call Granny, text, and Face-Time her regularly so she can see that we love her without us having to say it all the time. I'm not mushy, but I care about my

Granny a lot. I'm her oldest granddaughter. That's pretty cool to me because my Mom & Granny are their grandma's oldest granddaughters too. We have high standards to set apparently, not only are we the oldest but each of us has strong personalities and great leadership qualities.

It is crucial that your big sisters or other girls that you look up to are influencers or role models. And you have to be the same way for little girls that may be looking up to you. All growing girls need someone to look up to as a positive influence. We all have choices so why not choose to be the best. Your circle or your sisters should be able to do something better than you. You guys should be able to learn something from one another. My big sisters are strong, independent, beautiful, young, encouraging, and amazing girls. So, I'm all of those things for my little sisters to see too. I practice these qualities because I love myself. I have my days, and I'm not perfect but I'm strong, and I strive to be better every day no matter what. Love starts within, real genuine love anyway. Don't be afraid of love, or think that what I'm saying is too good to be true. There are good people around who want to love others and grow with them. In an ideal world, all girls can get along and cheer each other on no matter what. Just because nobody is perfect doesn't mean we can't try to be. I would love to be that girl who encourages and inspires her little sisters and maybe big ones 24/7, and only does things with a purpose. I want to make sure that I give inspiration to all little girls in the world. I want them to feel like they all are my real sisters because they are. Two of my favorite little cousins that are genuinely like my sisters are Tycen, and Aubree. I know I am oldest, but they also inspire me to keep encouraging them. I hope all my little sisters know how much I love them, and share the same vibes with their little sisters too!

Name a few sisters you listen to:

_____

_____

Who influences you and what have you learned from them?

_____

_____

Love is what it does. Do you tell your sisters that you love them more than you show?

_____

Chapter 3

Make New Friends But Keep The Old

Friend | 'frend |

One that favors or promotes something

Your life should consist of going to different places and meeting new people. It's so important not to forget the friends you have made as you grow, and remain open to making new ones. Sometimes having new friends means you can't keep some of your old friends. Your groups of friends may not compliment each other. Maybe you'll start to do different things that won't allow you to be the same as you were or even keep the same company. Never deal with a situation where one friend might not like your other friends and say they can't be your friend unless your not friends with the other person. You shouldn't have to pick or choose, and there are ways to be neutral so you can keep both. You have to be clear with your friends that you are not going to favor them because that's not fair to anyone involved. If you have a friend that wants to demand you choose between them and another friend, stand your ground girl, and you have to tell them you're not going to stop being friends with someone just because someone else does not like them. I've made a lot of friends & I've lost plenty too. Fortunately, the friends I've lost contact with was because my family moved so whenever I visit an old city or neighborhood I'll be happy to see some of the girls I used to know. Just because I don't live near my buddies doesn't mean we're not friends either.

Here's an example:

I attended Washington Montessori Elementary from pre-3 through 1st grade. My second-grade year my family moved into a house located outside of the city, so I had to change schools, and I attended

Wedgwood Elementary. I was able to keep some of my friends from Washington Montessori because we were on the same cheer team at Herbert Hoover Boys & Girls Club of Saint Louis, and others I was able to exchange contact information with. Recently my family moved again from St Louis, Mo to Houston, Texas. Now I am a third grader at Outley Elementary. Can you imagine all the friends I've made, and lost during these transitions? I don't like going to different schools, but I love meeting new people and learning different things from them. I am sad sometimes about my friends that I don't talk to anymore, but I'll always remember them, and I'm sure that they'll think of me. Some friends don't stay close, so you forget about them because they're not around. You may be waiting to see them, or so much time will pass that they just become old friends you once knew. So what I do is keep a phone book, and I stay in contact with my close friends no matter where I live or where I may be in the future.

I have made lots of friends since we've moved to Houston, some enemies too. One of my classmates said that we were friendemies, but I don't do the half and half situations, so I told her what she didn't want to hear. I'm sharing that because I have to be honest with you guys. Being true to yourself and others is necessary. You won't want to treat every girl you meet as a sister, how about letting them bond with someone who does want to treat them that way. Don't be fake or rude about it, but be fair. Time is valuable, and life is short so be the best sister that you know how to be as much as you can. None of us is perfect but being ugly to others says a lot about how much you love yourself. Sometimes making friends can put you in dangerous situations with others. When you make friends, they may be the wrong ones, and some friends can get you into a lot of trouble, so you need to be careful who you think is your friend at school or anywhere else. Lots of people do the wrong things, and it's okay to make mistakes because to every problem there's a solution, but be careful to not make friends with people that make a lot of confusion. Friendship can be a journey to lots of different places so before you have friends you have to ask yourself are you ready for this next adventure of your life. Some people stay with you forever, and some people move on. Figure out who you want to stay, and be as good of a friend that you expect others to be so they're never too far for you to reach. I don't think I'll ever have a problem keeping old friends because I'm honest, focused, social, I pay attention, and what needs to be done I do. I don't mean to toot my own horn, but those are all great qualities of a friend!

Name:

Number:

Address:

Birthday:

Sisters since:

Name:

Number:

Address:

Birthday:

Sisters since:

Name:

Number:

Address:

Birthday:

Sisters since:

Name:

Number:

Address:

Birthday:

Sisters since:

Name:

Number:

Address:

Birthday:

Sisters since:

Name:

Number:

Address:

Birthday:

Sisters since:

Chapter 4

Love Yourself Girl Or Nobody Will

Self Love | ′self•lev |

Regard for one's own well-being and happiness.

To have self-love, you need self-respect. If you do not love and respect yourself, you will not be able to do it to someone else, and people will not know the way you want them to treat you. Self-love and self-respect are alike because loving, and respecting both mean you have to take care of yourself and treat yourself especially good. The way you want others to treat you is your choice. You should always make loving yourself essential. If you like a person more than yourself, that means you don't appreciate the things you do for them because you're the one doing it, that's not right. It's good to love yourself more because all the things you do for others can take hard work, so you need love to be the best you to get the job done. Ask yourself what makes you have self-love and why you respect yourself? You should make sure people you are sharing your acts of kindness with are deserving of what makes you treat yourself with love before you treat them with the same. There are many reasons people show self-love one of mine is to give myself a special treat for all the hard work I do. Sister, if you do not respect yourself, no one will respect you at all. Trust me; we are all human and more than likely we will all go through similar things. You have more in common with sisters that you don't know that you may think. One thing we all should work to have is self-love. Even if you're having a bad day, you'll be able to think of something about yourself that you love. Loving and respecting ourselves is a good thing to do, it might sound selfish, but it's just giving a reward to yourself for doing the best you can all the time. You should always treat yourself right and others, but you still love yourself first.

    I care for myself by making sure I always treat myself to something sweet every so often. There are many ways to treat yourself to make sure you feel right about being you. Things like snacking, being at the mall, and spa activities are my favorite. My Granny bought me a pedicure tub that has a massage feature, and I use it at least once a month. I'll find some space that I can have to myself, lay down some towels, grab a chair, and relax. I have all the tools I need to scrub my heels, shape my nails, and polish too. It's my absolute most favorite thing to do! Ask your parents about things done in your culture, or a friend's lifestyle, and you'll discover many more ways to treat yourself too. I'll take a spa day any day.

Be nonchalant sometimes, when you're rewarding yourself. This way nobody will bother you while you're focused on self-love. Sometimes I'm so focused on myself that even the people in my house don't know what I'm doing. I don't share my alone time I'm very selfish with that. I don't need to share everything I'm doing for myself with anyone, because then am I doing it for others or me? I share with my sisters later when I'm showing off my pretty polish and smooth skin. If I ever wanted to relax and my sisters know it, they may ask me if I want a spa day because they know how I like to treat myself, and I never had to tell them because love is what it does (I showed them).

I used to forget to put my scarf on at night. My mom would have to replace my sisters and my scarves and bonnets a lot. It was like our bed sheets were eating them. My mom started buying satin pillowcases because she was out of ideas for places we should keep our scarves and bonnets. Mom probably wanted to save some money too. It wasn't far in between that my mom would still buy us more hair protection anyway. I'm glad she did this because she showed me how necessary it is to take care of my hair. Being able to manage natural hair is very important. I noticed that when I started to love my hair that my curl pattern was softer, and looser because I had gone from letting my hair break off from leaving it on cotton sheets to protecting my hair with delicate hair wrap. That was simple and easy. I was cautious and, I loved the new look too! We were able to cut back on the going to the salon because we take better care of ourselves. Anything you do with love will turn out great. Think about it; you shouldn't just feel good when you're leaving a salon or spa. You should know how to make yourself look and have the same sense of importance as your favorite professional people know how. What's the difference in them loving what they are doing for you, and you can do the same thing? There is no difference. Be careful of what food, and thoughts you put into your body. Has anyone ever told you that too much of anything isn't right for you? Well, it's true. So recently I've been craving a chocolate candy bar. So much that every time my mom goes to the store I ask her to bring me one back. My mom goes to the store every day. Because my mom likes to treat me, and she thinks that I deserve what I want she brings me back a candy bar every day. Self-care gets tricky. My mom knows what I like, and she wants me to feel special, so she buys me chocolate candy bars. My mom is also very serious about health and fitness but to make me feel good, she's giving me what I like. You have to remember to take care of yourself even when someone else forgets to do it for you. My mom loves me, but she wants to spoil me, and that probably had something to do with her buying all those candy bars. Plus she's so busy that if I ask her something she'll do things for me without thinking about what I say. I have to make sure I look out for me. My diet is important. I went to the doctor and even though my mom is the one buying all these candy bars she told my doctor that I wouldn't stop eating them. I couldn't believe it. My doctor said I could see a nutritionist, but my mom knows a lot about health and wellness so she promised her that we would do better. I think she just needed to slow down to realize what was going on but in all fairness, if I were better with my diet, my mom never would have bought those candy bars. It's easy to teach people how to treat you, love yourself.

Chapter 5

Black Girl Magic

| blak | gurl | maj•ik |

An expression created to uplift, encourage and celebrate the awesomeness of women of color.

I can do anything. Nothing I want is beyond my reach. I'm an 11-year-old African American girl who was raised by just my mom since I was two years old in St. Louis, MO. I'm an honor student at my school, and I plan on attending Spelman College or Howard University. I love to read, dance, acting, and anything that has to do with fun, beauty, and fashion! The summer of 2014 my sisters and I attended our second model call hosted by Lillian Tiner of LAHA. My sisters and I were a little nervous because we were in a room full of so many girls that were there with the same plan that we had, and that was to be selected to walk. Most girls had experience, and everyone was dressed to impress with their moms cheering them on and coaching them to be great. It would be Dumia's first time auditioning to walk in a fashion show, but she seemed to be the least nervous of us all. We shouldn't have been worried at all but some things you can do a billion times and still get butterflies when you're asked to present in front of a live audience. Ms. Lillian coached the girls and me every Saturday morning to prepare to walk in her up and coming Runway Fashion Show. She's the best. Ms. Lillian and her team trained so many girls that were ages six and older. I believe that she was so good; she could probably work with us with her eyes closed. The training taught me to be confident and focus. It's easy to be distracted when so many people surround you. Sometimes you're thinking about what someone else is doing, or you're just being a kid and having a blast because what else should you do if you're in a room with fifty or more other girls. My mom would always say have fun, but then she'd also say this is serious and it's not fair to waste anyone's time. We were instructed to be on our best behavior and do what we came to do, be our best. We had a good show, and the other girls expressed the same excitement. Ms. Lillian's shows were like something you would see on television. That's why I would never forget the next time Ms. Lillian called us to return.

The following year my mom bought me a sewing machine and signed me up at a summer sewing camp in the Arts District. I had great fun! The center was full of creative girls who had so many other talents than sewing! We sang, danced, and put on fashion shows wearing each other's work. My mom was so proud that she would take pictures every time I stitched a button and post it on the Internet. Lucky for me those pictures got Ms. Lillian's attention, and she invited me to be a designer in her 2016 I Have a Dream Runway Show! This invitation was the most significant thing a girl my age could hope to do! I still love Ms. Lillian for giving me the opportunity of a lifetime. So, of course, I had my sisters' model for me, and I was able to pick six other models too. I decided to name my line Number 8 because that's my lucky number, and it was time for me to get to business. We woke up every Sat morning and went to rehearsal at the Kappa House on Vandeventer only this time I wasn't rehearsing. Can you imagine a nine-year-old seamstress getting models ready to wear her designs? It felt like a dream. When I remember the show, I get so excited, and it takes my breath away. Finally, January 16 came, and it was show time. I was ready to put all of my models into their outfits. I had been fortunate to have my Granny provide her expert help in the sewing area. It was enjoyable because all of my friends and family were there to support me and go through the journey along with me that day. Some people came backstage to wish me luck and more. I had walked in shows for many of the designers backstage too. When I had the final walk with my models, my world changed. I get what my mom was talking about when she used to say to me "Dakai you're not average." That was one of two fashion shows that I got to feature in that year and I was very honored both times. I went from being nervous to walk for designers, to having models grace the stage for me. That felt like magic! I never thought about designing clothes, I started playing dress up one day and thought I was destined to model them.

All girls have something unique about them. When you take whatever that is and apply lots of love to it, magic happens!

I still have my sewing machine. In fact, I have 3. My sisters are still getting this magic!

Circle your answer below:

Do you believe in yourself?

YES   IDK   NO

Do you express what's unique about you?

YES   IDK   NO

Does someone influence you?

YES   IDK   NO

What profession do you plan to pursue?

_____

Are you a part of a group or an organization that is helping to make you better at what you love to do?

_____

Chapter 6

Want to Win

Win | win |

To gain victory: succeed.

Sister, if you're going to do something small don't do it at all. Go for the big win no matter what you're trying to pursue. You can do everything you put your mind to do. You have to believe that you can achieve anything because you can. Trust is an essential factor when you are trying new things. The more you trust that you deserve great things you can be confident to achieve them. Believe it or not, I can't remember one time that I didn't trust myself to do my very best and for that reason if I tried out for a part, and didn't get it or whatever the case may have been I could accept it with a smile and consider it practice. There is forever room for improvement, never forget that. My motto is if you believe it you can achieve it.

I'm on the step team at my school. One time there was an opportunity to compete for a rap feature in a performance. I was so determined to get this part because whoever won would have a chance to rap a song wrote by my step instructor, and we would be rapping with our school principal at two of our elementary school awards ceremonies. For practice, I tried to be the first in the door and the last to leave. We had to rehearse before school some days, and I would have to wake my brother up 30 minutes earlier than usual to walk me across the street to school. He would get so mad at me because he likes to sleep until the very last minute before his bus arrives. I didn't care if I had to rehearse this routine a thousand times I had to earn this solo.

It was a lot for me to feel like I was competing with my teammates to get a solo part but I had to focus on my only goal. I wanted to perform the solo and if I didn't put forth my best effort that never would have happened. There was nothing personal against any of the girls on the step team. I wanted to display the best performance strictly for me! I can be very competitive, but I also know very well how to be a good team member. I always remember that each teammates position is as important as another to operate as one. No matter what my job was, my coach and the girls could count on me to get my part done. There are nine of us on the team, and we are all awesome! I knew that this would be a tough one because we all try our very best. We got the lyrics two weeks before the show. There were three verses so two people had the chance to win and Dr. Newby would be rapping the third verse. The auditioning day came, and I was very nervous. Three of my peers went before me and performed the first verse. When it was my turn, I chose to do both parts because I didn't know which one I would do better. We all cheered each other on but as I performed it seemed that my teammates were a little louder. My principal was there, and she gave me a high five when I finished. Everyone loved me. At first, Ms. Hutchinson said that the decision would be tough, but before practice was over, she told me that I had the part that I wanted.

It was the day to perform, and I was so confident that I was going to be great because I had practiced before, and after school to prepare myself mentally. I had the routine down packed. As we entered the gym, the school welcomed us with loud cheers, and we could hear Dr. Newby saying to our peers to clap it up for us. When it was time for my solo, I was so into it that my microphone screeched as soon as I opened my mouth because my voice is thunderous. I quickly adjusted my headset and continued like nothing was wrong because it wasn't. I figured that could have happened to anyone and we worked way too hard to throw our entire performance because of that. Afterward, we received so many congrats, and the show was so entertaining to our friends that nobody even mentioned the microphone incident. We rocked, and we knew it! Embarrassment is not an option. As young ladies, we face many challenges and stereotypes. As long as you're determined you can do anything you set your mind to do. Always set goals, focus, and work towards improving your skills to be impeccable. The next day we performed again, and I know that we stepped better than the day before. We were so excited to show off what we practiced, and we showed it well! Both times we performed I tried to be better than I was at tryouts. If I could be better than I was the day I tried out for the solo I know that I would for sure be amazing every time. I'm a precocious girl; I don't even surprise myself anymore. Ultimately I'll always be a winner because that's what I want.

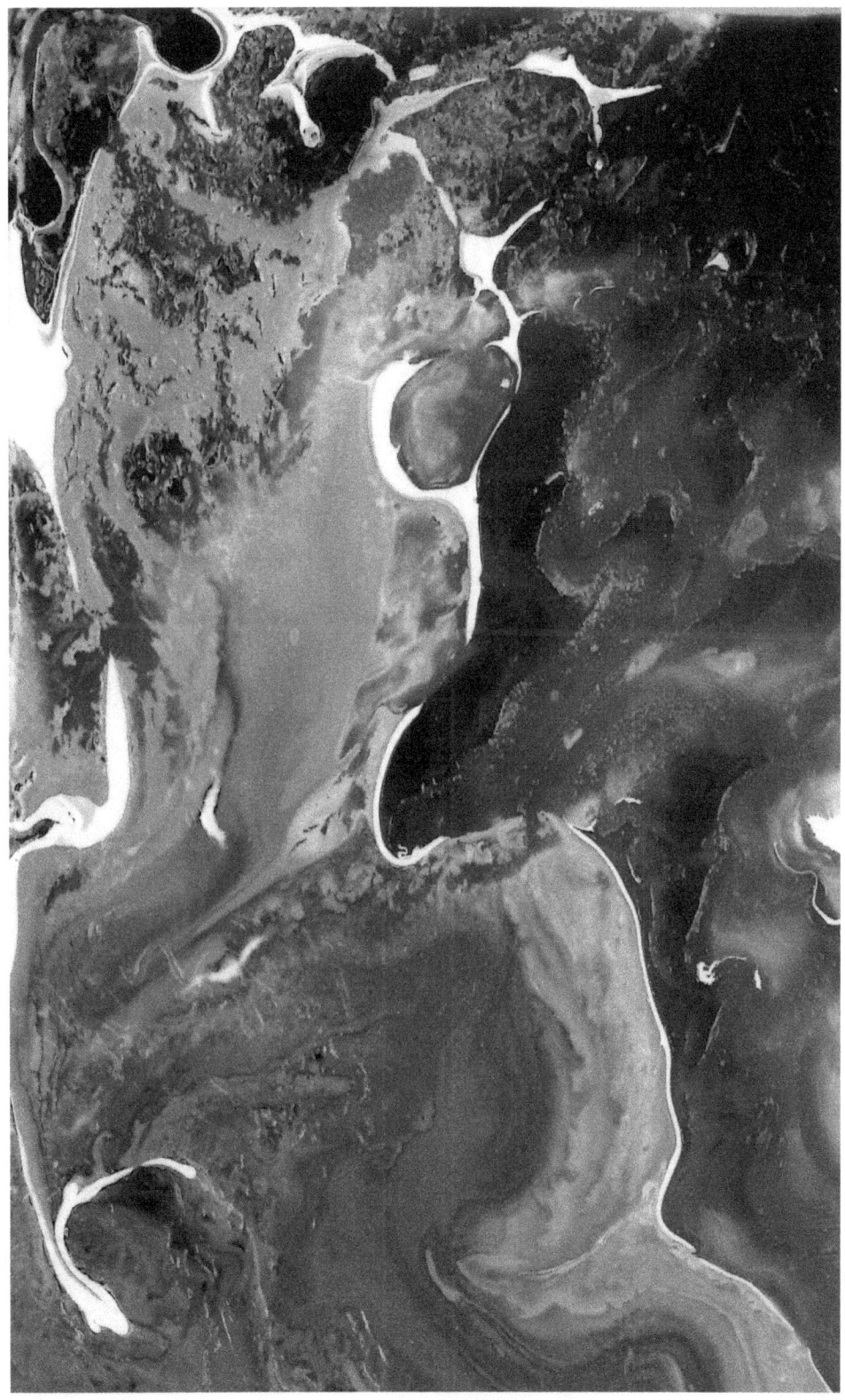

Chapter 7

A Valuable Lesson

Value | ʹvalyōō |

Estimate the monetary worth of (something)

Patience | pa-SHens |

To accept or tolerate delay, or troubles, without getting angry or upset.

Invest | inʹvest |

The act of committing money or capital to an endeavor with the expectation of obtaining an additional income or profit.

My mom bought each of us a limited edition Princess Tiana Doll for Christmas about six years ago. We ended up with two each because our Pa-Pa Ducey bought us one too. Our mom didn't allow us to open the dolls because she said they were collector's items. The toy was unique to my mom because not only was she the ninth Disney Princess, Tiana is the first African-American princess. We put them on shelves in our room, and they collected dust! We were ages three, four, and five when Mom and Pa-Pa purchased our dolls; they were $50 each. The lesson:

Six years later we found our dolls at our Granny's house, still in the boxes, undamaged. Granny decided to talk with us about how things become valuable.

She looked up the price of what our dolls were currently worth and wow was I surprised! The listed value of our six-year-old toys was $300 each unopened, but $30 out of the package. We were all talking about what would happen if we opened them and the more we discussed the baby dolls, the more anxious I got. I couldn't wait for a second longer to open mine. My sisters thought I was crazy, my Granny didn't agree with my decision, but I wanted to play with my doll. I never once stopped to imagine how much more my baby doll could be worth in six more years. Granny called and told my mom what I did, and she was furious. I didn't know why my mom wanted us to leave our dolls alone. I didn't even believe that the baby dolls gained value because they were toys. Mom told my sisters and I a few times they would be worth more if we kept them for a while, but I still didn't understand how. My Granny was teaching me a lesson by letting me choose for myself if the Tiana doll was more important to me in or out of the box. If I would have listened to anything I was told, I'm sure I would have got to hear how or why the value went up but I was too busy trying to open the only doll that I wasn't allowed to hold. Then, I learned the importance of investing, and to be patient. I think the real lesson was that I should listen. Now I have a Tiana worth $30, and one worth $300. I wish that I wouldn't have opened my doll because I could have sold both of them for way more than what my mom paid for them. My sisters didn't make matters well, they just kept bragging about how if we sold our dolls right then they would each have $600, and I'd be looking at $330. I wish I could have been patient. Nowadays I'm working on that character quality. I could have even sold one doll and bought another to play with and maybe ended up with $550 instead of $330. The point is I was so excited I didn't think twice about a decision that I wouldn't be able to change. Money doesn't grow on trees. I think it should, but since it doesn't, it's important to save and invest whenever you can. It's also important to listen, learn, and think before you act. I still have my doll because I believe that maybe some little girl will be happy to have her. Just because I removed her from her box doesn't take away from the fact she's still the first African American princess. It drives my mom nuts to see me sitting outside with Tiana. I'll try to never make this type of mistake ever again in my life because my sisters made me feel sorry for it and it doesn't feel right to take a loss either. I'm just a kid, but practice makes perfect. Also, to be a young lady and own valuable things is something to be very proud of. It's a luxury. I'll listen next time, and try to make the right decision instead of doing immature things. I never needed to open the doll anyway; I have tons of toys. I'm so used to sharing things with my sisters. If I got it, they got it. Dumia and I share a room. We go to school together, we're on some of the same teams, and every time one of us gets something so do the others except the colors are different. All these things made me want to open my doll even more. Finally, I had something that my sisters didn't have. We don't need to share everything. Dakai doesn't like sharing her clothes, Dumia doesn't like sharing her food, and I didn't want to share the thought of us collectively sitting on a gold mine. Well, now that I think about it I wish I didn't want to share something else because me losing out due to the way I felt didn't make sense. I intended to have something to myself, not to be foolish. With that being said think before you do things. Don't be so quick to do things just because you want to be different. Your sisters can be equal to you to a certain degree. You girls can outgrow each other too. Try not to be so different that you miss out on good things. We have to stick together, be patient, and be better with your sisters.

Chapter 8

Count Your Blessings

Blessed | blest |

Divinely or supremely favored; fortunate

When people are unique to you, show them. Everyone won't be born with loving parents, siblings, and of course not friends. It's a blessing to have people in your life that you don't have to teach how to love you they do it. It's also nice to know people that have that quality. It's so necessary to let people know how important they are to you. Sisters are emotional, sensitive, and should stay handled with care. Some people will always pay attention to the way we feel about things, and a lot of the time our feelings will rub off on them, or maybe not. When people change based off of the way you feel about things that's how you know they care, that's love.

My mom has been a single parent from 2008-2016. For a long while, my male role models were my brother Amir, cousins Anthony, Tony, and

Theo, uncles Kaleb, Anthony, Terrell, Seth, Moni, and my two Pa-Pas. They are my biggest blessings as far as men to look up to and love. My father died when I was two, and I don't know how. I don't think my mom will ever tell me. From what I've learned about my Dad he was very cool, and he and my mom had a perfect relationship. My Uncle Anthony, Kaleb, Anthony, and Tony have been my mom's support system throughout everything she's gone through raising Amir, the girls, and myself. My family constantly tells me how much I look like my dad, but my friends and other people that are close to me say I look like my mom. My Great Grandma would say "Girl, you look just like yo' Daddy." She said that every time I saw her. I would laugh or have this huge smile on my face. I have pictures in my room of my

Dad, and me. I also have a sister and four other brothers besides my mom's kids that were born before my sisters, and I was. I was fortunate to see my brothers almost every weekend before my family moved to Houston. We were on teams at the same sports centers, which made it easy for us to see them. I haven't got to see my sister Notti much because she's so much older than we are but every once in a while we say hello somehow. I know that our relationship is going to be awesome when time allows it to be. My Dad's family is supportive of everything I do, and whenever I see them, it's so much love expressed. My mom and my Aunt Charlie talk all the time. Considering everyone is living in a different state I appreciate that they are in contact. Recently my granny (Dad's mom) passed away.

In my mind, if you don't have your biological Dad or Mom in your life, you should always have at least someone to fill that role. Those people are blessings. Love isn't something that everyone knows how to do, so the people that God puts in your life that knows how to do it, let them and love them back genuinely. Since we aren't perfect sometimes, we forget things we shouldn't, for example even the most influential people need love. You have to love whoever loves you, that makes your life easier. The special people that I listed are a big deal to me and each of them has helped me become the daughter, sister, cousin, and overall ambitious, leading, compassionate girl I am today. These relationships have taught me to humbly except support, compliments, and constructive criticism at the same time. I wouldn't trade the people that my sisters and I were raised by for all my favorite things in the world. They are my blessings and I'm forever grateful for them. They all treat me like a daughter without ever mentioning it. My family, friends or peers never talk about my Dad passing away, but my sisters' classmates have said rude things to them. I think that happened to them because they shared personal things with people that they shouldn't have. I'm not sure how the conversations they were having even started, and I never asked because by the time they would make it home to tell me, and my mom what happened they were furious. We know how to turn a negative conversation into a positive one, so that makes me unsure why my sisters didn't take full control of their emotions. I have their backs all the time through good and whatever else. I get so sad when my sisters are hurt since I'm the oldest I never let them know that and I push them to be more robust.

I have never been sad about my Dad passing away because my Mom has done a lot to make sure that my siblings and I are happy and we have many great memories of Dad. I have an apparent understanding that everyone has to leave earth, and we have no idea when that will happen to us. My Dad not being with my family has made me very strong, and I know that I make my Dad proud and I will continue to do so with love.

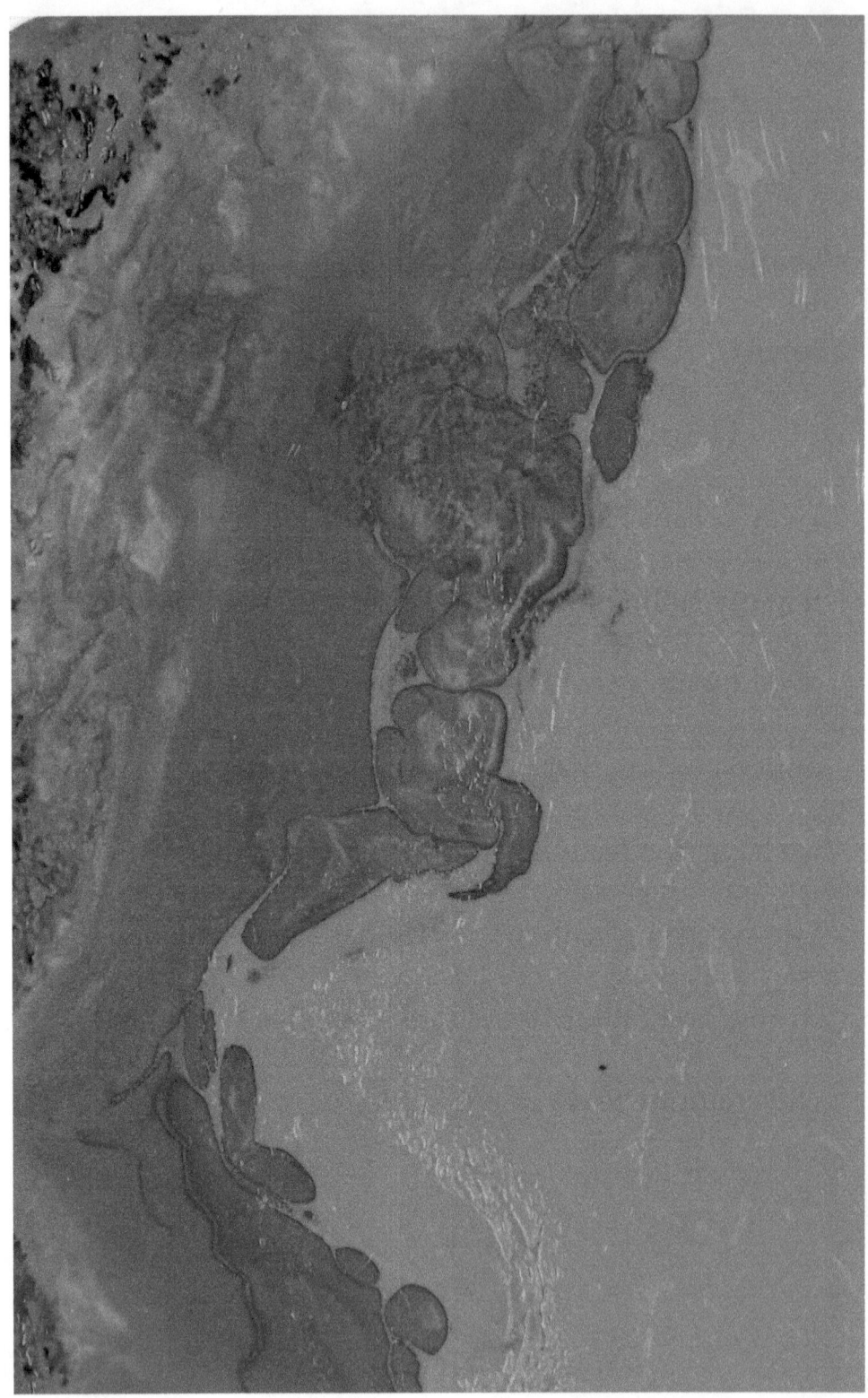

Chapter 9

Love The Skin You're In

Be-You-tiful

Be your best, beautiful self.

You shouldn't try to be someone that you're not, because it may require much more time and energy to be someone else. I am the middle sister; slimmer, darker, and my hair is short and curly, I'm the shortest in height. I have the brightest smile, I'm very animated, and I'm way more social than my sisters. I get frustrated when people ask if Dumia and I are twins because I think we look so different. Sometimes my mom confuses us too, but that's because we're close in height. I'm two inches smaller than my little sister. She's also passed me up in her clothes size. This works for me because she gets to wear Dakai's clothes instead of mine. My style is very different from my sisters, and I always express that, so we don't cross paths too often in the wardrobe area. We don't dress alike at all. Dakai likes to dress up, Dumia loves sporty looks, and I'm unique, so my style is edgy/chic. I don't try to impress, but I like to express.

My sisters and I all have different lengths of hair. We also have various curl patterns. As I mentioned earlier my hair is the shortest, but its soft, and curly. I take care of my hair with love, and it's very healthy. I can wear any style that I want that's appropriate for my hair length. Sometimes I wear my hair natural with braids, and other times I wear it blow dried straight. Dumia has spongy hair, but its super soft and has natural brown highlights. She loves to rock cornrows into different styles and puffballs. Dakai's hair stops in the middle of her back. She can practically wear any style she wants, but she's always last to get her hair styled at home.

I think Dakai is the reason our mom sends us to the salon because by the time it's Dakai's turn to be shampooed and styled everyone is tired of combing hair all day.

If I tried to be like Dakai, my eyes would regret it, but my heart would be all in. Dakai studies everything that she loves. She's a great dancer, but that bores me. I'm working on some new moves, but I would never try and keep up with Dakai. She's very competitive, and I'm not at all. Plenty of times, she teaches us dance routines, and she's like a drill sergeant. I loved to dance when we were younger, but now that we're older I'm interested in other things. However, I still have rhythm.

My interesting little sister Dumia has a vocabulary that's larger than some adults.

She's gifted, we all are, but Dumia is like a kid genius. I'm glad that I don't know all the words she does because I honestly think that most of the ones she uses are offensive. She told someone that her feet are sere, that means dry or lacking moisture. Dumia uses many of these words to be funny, but they are not to me. I could wish I was as smart as Dumia, but I'll pass on it. I try my best, and even though I don't know college words, I'm awarded an honor roll certificate every quarter.

Deep down you have to love everything about yourself. I realized that if you try to be someone else you could miss out on what could make you happy for the rest of your life. My sisters and I are best friends, but we'd rather be different to always have something unusual to share with each other.

Chapter 10

Honor The Code

Sister Code sis-ter • | kōd |

A system between two or more girls, not always related by blood. The girls support, trust, and love each other like sisters for purposes of a bond that should never be broken.

The Valley Girls are a package deal! I have fun with my sisters, I argue with my sisters, and I love them no matter what. I love my sisters, even though they seldom make me mad. I found out before I was old enough to leave the house what it was like to create healthy relationships with other girls. Being raised in a home with two sisters, my mom, and having a large family with plenty of aunts and cousins I got the opportunity to see females treat each other many ways. From that, I learned that the better you treat people, the better they will treat you. If I care for people that I love like I treat my blood sisters that says a lot about how genuine I am. When my sisters and I argue our mom has us do small things together that are annoying and that makes us wish we never even disagreed.

I've learned that she does that because we can get way more accomplished with each other together than we can apart, and she doesn't ever want us to forget that. I'm grateful that I have my sisters to do so many things with. They are my first, and best friends. They know me better than I know myself sometimes because people can see more of us than we can. I don't expect my sisters to agree with me always, but I do hope they remain loyal, supportive, and honest. We're taught to put in work with your sisters. Use them and let them use you. If you can't come together and help or be helped with a pure heart, you're not ready for sisterhood.

Honoring the sister code is what makes you a good sister. People will try you, that shouldn't be your problem. Stay true to who you are, and focus on being great. Focus on your sisters who want to be great too because you guys can be helpful to one another. Educate your sisters that need it. Remember that some people don't know how to be kind to others, but you cant allow yourself to be pulled in by people who don't have the same beliefs and goals as you have and are not trying to change. It could be that they aren't ready to improve too, in that case, you can move on respectfully. Respect yourself and others always.

I think it's significant to raise awareness for girls who don't know that they are front page worthy. There have to be more girls that want to see other girls win. We have to support each other, and we should show love to each other. That should be law.

As girls, we are judged enough for every little thing that we do. We shouldn't judge each other because nobody is perfect. I think that people expect so much from us and sometimes we forget we set the bar. You have to have good qualities and remain confident, not weak. That sums up the sister code.

Dear Diya,

You're the best! And I'm glad to be able to share everything we experience with you. The world wouldn't be sweet without sisters! Everyone has them in God's eyes, and I'm blessed with three, you, Notti, and Dumia. I hope you know I'm so proud of how ambitious you are. I expect to watch you become a beautiful actress, print model, singer, and maybe dancer. I also hope I'm setting a great example of what an older sister should be, and when I'm not, you should let me know so I can change that (big sisters need love too). Always help our little sister as I help you. If you ever feel like I don't have your back, remember I'm not perfect, and I'll change almost whatever to make us closer.

We argue right? In all honesty that shows signs of love. Only someone determined to help a person should be arguing. There's nothing wrong with sisters doing that, but you have to know when to draw the line. Don't be too catty. Avoid unnecessary altercations. Always put forth your best effort in making sure you show your little sister what a fabulous big sister should be. Be respectful, realistic, be confident, be a friend and mentor. Always have Faith, Loyalty, Hope, and Honesty. United we can accomplish so much.

With Peace & Love,

Kai

Dear Dumia,

I know we don't get to talk about our feelings a lot, but I want you to know that I love you and even if you and I argue and fight that won't change anything. If I have said some mean and hurtful things before I am sorry for that and you know I am because you're my one & only favorite little sister! I want our sister-relationship to be better than it was before I made this letter to you. I love you little sister with all my heart.

With Love,

Diya

Dear Little Sisters,

Even though I'm your big sister, you show me a lot too. Thank you for looking up to me. I'm honored to be someone that you trust. Life gets crazy but knowing that I have you watching me gives me so much motivation to make good choices. I encourage you always to do your best and work very hard to achieve your goals. As long as you do things with love you will be successful. Be brave and never forget that you can do anything you imagine. Thank you for being my sister. Thanks for growing, sharing, and sticking to the sister code with me. We are sisters for life, so know that I always got your back. I'll love you know matter what path you choose to follow.

Sisters have to show each other understanding, and I'll be around if you need me girl!

With Love,

Dumia

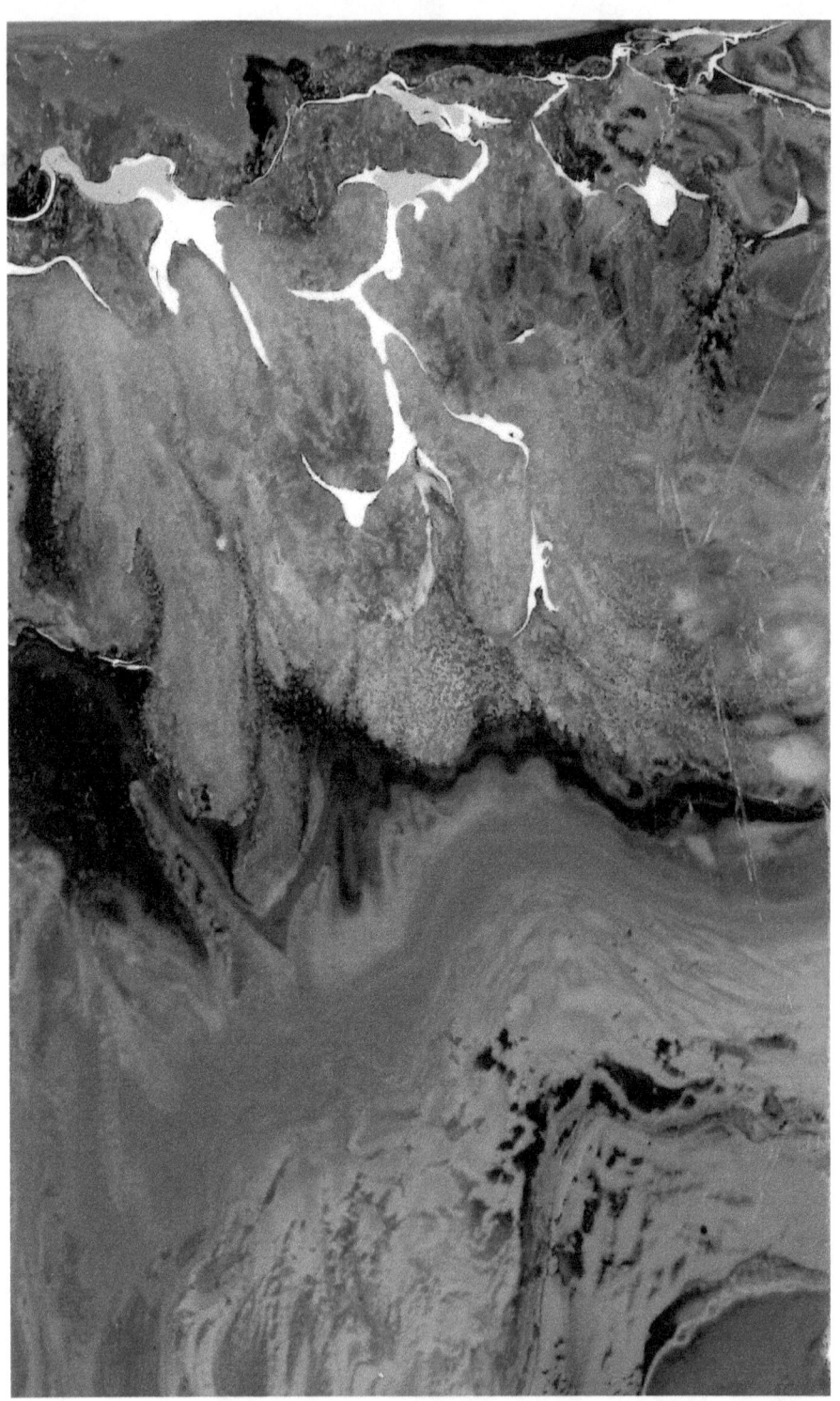

www.ingramcontent.com/pod-product-compliance
Lightning Source LLC
Chambersburg PA
CBHW071744090426
42738CB00011B/2555